EXPLORING COUNTRIES

Haiti

BLAINE WISEMAN

www.av2books.com

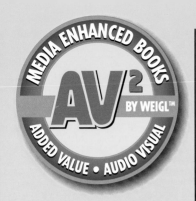

AV² provides enriched content that supplements and complements this book. Weigl's AV² books strive to create inspired learning and engage young minds in a total learning experience.

Your AV² Media Enhanced books come alive with...

Audio
Listen to sections of the book read aloud.

Key Words
Study vocabulary, and complete a matching word activity.

Go to **www.av2books.com**, and enter this book's unique code.

Video
Watch informative video clips.

Quizzes
Test your knowledge.

BOOK CODE

R 4 6 6 3 9 8

Embedded Weblinks
Gain additional information for research.

Slide Show
View images and captions, and prepare a presentation.

AV² by Weigl brings you media enhanced books that support active learning.

Try This!
Complete activities and hands-on experiments.

... and much, much more!

Published by AV² by Weigl
350 5th Avenue, 59th Floor
New York, NY 10118
Website: www.av2books.com

Library of Congress Cataloging-in-Publication Data

Names: Wiseman, Blaine, author.
Title: Haiti / Blaine Wiseman.
Description: New York, NY : AV2 by Weigl, [2017] | Series: Exploring
    countries | Includes index.
Identifiers: LCCN 2016047213 (print) | LCCN 2016047910 (ebook) | ISBN
    9781489660794 (hard cover : alk. paper) | ISBN 9781489660800 (soft cover :
    alk. paper) | ISBN 9781489660817 (Multi-user ebk.)
Subjects: LCSH: Haiti—Juvenile literature.
Classification: LCC F1915.2 .W57 2017 (print) | LCC F1915.2 (ebook) | DDC
    972.94—dc23

Printed in the United States of America in Brainerd, Minnesota
1 2 3 4 5 6 7 8 9 21 20 19 18 17

022017
020117

Project Coordinator Heather Kissock
Art Director Terry Paulhus

Photo Credits
Every reasonable effort has been made to trace ownership and to obtain permission to reprint copyright material. The publishers would be pleased to have any errors or omissions brought to their attention so that they may be corrected in subsequent printings.

Weigl acknowledges Getty Images as its primary photo supplier for this title.

Contents

Haiti Overview

The country of Haiti is located in the Caribbean Sea, off the southeastern coast of mainland North America. Most of the country covers the western one-third of the island of Hispaniola. Several smaller islands are also part of Haiti. The country has rugged mountains, long coastlines, and broad **plains**. During its history, people from many regions have helped form Haiti's culture. Today, Haiti's landscapes and people make it an exciting country to explore.

The rhinoceros iguana, which grows to about 2 feet (0.6 meters) long, is found only on Hispaniola.

Some Haitians bring vegetables they have grown to public markets to sell.

Mountain ranges extend to the sea in parts of Haiti's long coastline.

Tap-taps are decorated buses that provide transport throughout Haiti.

Soccer is a popular sport among Haiti's children.

Exploring Haiti

Haiti covers 10,750 square miles (27,800 square kilometers). It is the third-largest Caribbean country. Haiti has only one land border, with the Dominican Republic to the east. Cuba lies 50 miles (80 kilometers) northwest of Haiti, and Jamaica is 120 miles (190 km) west. Cuba, Hispaniola, and Jamaica are part of an archipelago, or group of islands, called the Greater Antilles.

Massif du Nord

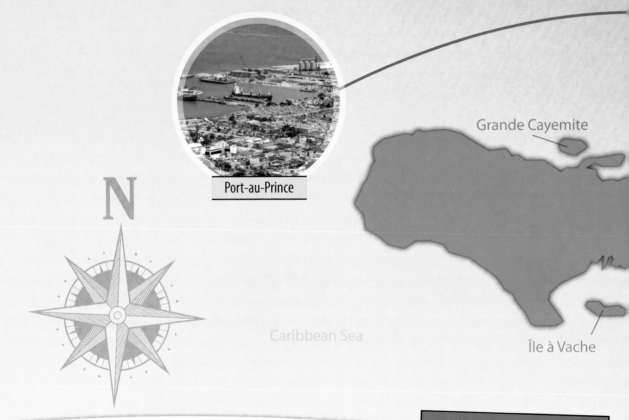
Port-au-Prince

Grande Cayemite

N

Caribbean Sea

Île à Vache

Map Legend

 Haiti

Land

Water

 Massif du Nord

Artibonite River

Lake Azuei

Capital City

SCALE

30 Miles

30 Kilometers

Port-au-Prince

Port-au-Prince is the capital city of Haiti. It is located at the edge of the Bay of Port-au-Prince. The city was founded in 1749, and it became Haiti's capital in 1770.

Tortuga

Atlantic Ocean

Gulf of
Gonâve

HAITI

Artibonite River

Île de la
Gonâve

Dominican
Republic

Bay of
Port-au-Prince

Port-au-Prince

Lake Azuei

Massif du Nord

In the northern part of Haiti lies a mountain range called the Massif du Nord. The name means "northern mountains." It runs east–west and extends into the Dominican Republic.

Artibonite River

The Artibonite River is the country's longest river. It is about 175 miles (280 km) long. The river begins in the western part of the Dominican Republic and flows southwest along the border with Haiti. The Artibonite then flows west through Haiti and empties into the Gulf of Gonâve.

Lake Azuei

Eleven miles (18 km) east of Port-au-Prince is Lake Azuei, also known as Lake Saumâtre. The lake covers about 65 square miles (170 sq. km) and reaches to the border with the Dominican Republic. It is Haiti's largest lake.

LAND AND CLIMATE

Mainland Haiti, the part of the country on Hispaniola, has three major regions. These are the northern, central, and southern regions. In addition, Haiti has four main offshore islands. Tortuga is to the north. Île de la Gonâve is in the Gulf of Gonâve. Île à Vache and Grande Cayemite are off the southwestern coast.

The west side of mainland Haiti has two long **peninsulas**, located north and south of the Gulf of Gonâve. To the northwest of the northern peninsula is the Windward Passage. This is a **strait** where the Atlantic Ocean and the Caribbean Sea meet.

In mainland Haiti's northern region, the Massif du Nord stretches westward through the entire northern peninsula. The northern plain is also part of the northern region. It lies between the Massif du Nord and Haiti's north coast.

A number of Haiti's small islands are made up largely of coral reefs.

The central region includes mountain ranges and areas of flat land. The Central **Plateau** is south of the Massif du Nord. The Montagnes Noires mountain range lies southwest of this plateau. The Artibonite Plain extends across the central region in the area around the Artibonite River. To the south of this plain are the mountain ranges called the Chaine des Matheux and the Montagnes du Trou d'Eau.

In Haiti's southern region, the Cul-de-Sac Plain extends from Port-au-Prince Bay in the west to the border of the Dominican Republic in the east. Two mountain ranges, the Massif de la Selle in the east and the Massif de la Hotte in the west, are found in southern Haiti. Pic la Selle, Haiti's tallest peak, is part of the Massif de la Selle mountain range.

Haiti has a tropical climate, with hot and humid weather year-round. The heaviest rainfall occurs from February to May. Average high temperatures range from the high 70s Fahrenheit (about 25° Celsius) in January and February to the mid-90s Fahrenheit (about 35°C) in July and August. Haiti is in a region that is often hit by hurricanes in summer and fall.

Land and Climate BY THE NUMBERS

1,098 Miles
Length of Haiti's coastline. (1,767 km)

More Than 2 Million
Number of Haitians affected by damage from Hurricane Matthew in October 2016.

8,793 Feet
Height of Pic la Selle. (2,680 m)

Forests cover some mountainous regions in southern Haiti.

PLANTS AND ANIMALS

Haiti's tropical climate provides good growing conditions for many types of plants. In the past, much of the country was covered by forests. However, most of Haiti's forests have been cut down, to use the wood and to make room for farms and settlements. Still common today are the royal palm trees that line Haiti's beaches.

A wide variety of animals live in Haiti, including more than 300 **species** of birds. The Hispaniolan trogan is Haiti's national bird. Reptiles found in Haiti include snakes, crocodiles, and caimans, as well as iguanas.

Haiti is home to some **mammals** found only in the Caribbean. The solenodon is a small rodent with a long snout that mainly eats other small animals. It uses venom, a poisonous substance, in its saliva to kill animals that it bites. Hutias use their long claws for climbing. These rodents build nests in trees and feed on leaves. Both solenodons and hutias are **endangered**. They are hunted as pests and have lost much of their **habitat**.

27 Number of species of snakes in Haiti.

5% Portion of Haiti's land that is forested today.

UP TO 60 FEET
Height to which royal palm trees can grow. (18 m)

In recent centuries, Haiti has lost about 98 percent of its natural forests.

NATURAL RESOURCES

Haiti is not rich in natural resources. Mining has largely depleted, or used up, the country's deposits of minerals such as gold, copper, and **bauxite**. Some gold and copper mining continues in northern Haiti, and international mining companies are searching for new deposits.

Wood from Haiti's remaining forests is an important source of fuel. Outside the Port-au-Prince area, most Haitians do not have electricity in their homes. They use wood or charcoal, which is made from wood, for cooking, lighting, and heating. Firewood and charcoal make up almost three-fourths of the fuel used in Haiti.

1982 Year Haiti's last major bauxite mine closed.

30 Million
Number of trees used each year to make charcoal.

1971 Year the Péligre Dam's hydroelectric plant was completed.

The country's rivers are used to produce **hydroelectricity**. However, power outages occur when hot, dry weather causes low river water levels. On the other hand, hydroelectric facilities such as the Péligre Dam on the Artibonite River help control flooding during wet weather in the Artibonite Plain. The plain's rich soil makes it an important crop-growing area.

The Péligre Dam supplies about one-third of the country's electricity.

TOURISM

About 300,000 tourists visit Haiti each year. Visitors can see historic sites, beautiful natural areas, and a variety of sea life in coastal waters. A growing trend is to visit Haiti as a volunteer. Such visitors help local people build homes and schools. This type of tourism has increased since a 2010 earthquake caused severe damage in Haiti.

Colorful fish and corals off Haiti's south coast are an attraction for snorkelers and divers.

In Port-au-Prince, the Musée du Panthéon National Haïtien (MUPANAH) is the city's most popular attraction. The museum's main building is a **mausoleum** that holds the remains of people who played important roles in Haiti's history. The museum has many historical **artifacts**. Shackles and chains that held African slaves brought to Haiti are displayed alongside crowns worn by rulers of the area. One of the MUPANAH's most notable artifacts is the anchor from the *Santa Maria*, the ship Christopher Columbus sailed on to reach the Caribbean in 1492.

The circular design at the center of the MUPANAH museum is based on the houses of the Taíno people, who were living on Hispaniola when Europeans arrived.

The northwest coast of Haiti is home to some of the country's most beautiful scenery and buildings. Haiti's National History Park contains the Sans-Souci Palace and the Citadelle Laferriere. These structures were built in the 1800s. The Citadelle is the largest fortress in North and South America. It was built to protect Haiti against attacks from the sea. Sans-Souci was the palace of Haiti's first king. The name means "without worry" in French.

Nearby, on the north coast, Labadee is home to a large dock for cruise ships. These ships carry thousands of tourists to Haiti each year. From the cruise ship dock, visitors can shop in local markets or take trips on small boats past shipwrecks and coral reefs. Labadee is known for its clear water and sandy beaches. Tourists can sunbathe, dive, or snorkel. A water playground is also popular.

On the south coast, Jacmel is another popular destination. The town is known for its beach and for its buildings in the style used in France during the 18th century. Nearby, Le Bassin-Bleu, or the Blue Basin, features waterfalls and **lagoons**.

Tourism BY THE NUMBERS

1982 Year the United Nations named the National History Park a **UNESCO** World Heritage site.

About 45,000 Number of Haitian jobs related to tourism.

2009 Year the port at Labadee was improved to allow the largest cruise ships to dock there.

The Sans-Souci Palace, completed in 1813, was originally surrounded by gardens and fountains. It was abandoned in 1820, after the king who built it died.

INDUSTRY

A griculture is one of Haiti's most important industries. Many Haitians depend on crops from **subsistence farming** to survive. Other farms produce crops to be sold. Haiti's main agricultural products are mangoes, coffee beans, sugarcane, rice, and corn. The country also produces sorghum, which is used to make molasses.

About 20 percent of Haiti's **gross domestic product** (GDP) comes from manufacturing. Some Haitian factories process the country's agricultural products, such as coffee beans or sugarcane. Other factories assemble **imported** parts or raw materials into finished goods. Manufacturing clothing is a major industry in Haiti. Clothing factories turn imported fabrics into products including T-shirts and jeans.

Clothing factories produce one-half of Haiti's manufactured goods.

Industry BY THE NUMBERS

38% Portion of Haitian workers engaged in agriculture.

126,000 Tons
Amount of rice, on average, grown in Haiti each year.
(114,000 metric tons)

$19 Billion
Size of Haiti's GDP.

GOODS AND SERVICES

Service industries make up the largest part of Haiti's economy. About one-half of Haitians have service jobs. People in such jobs provide services to others rather than produce goods. Service workers include teachers, truck drivers, mechanics, and salespeople.

A large number of Haitians cannot find full-time jobs. Many of these people work in what is called the informal economy. They accept work on a day-to-day basis, often performing tasks that require little training. Much of this work is in construction.

Although many Haitians work in agriculture, food is still Haiti's biggest import. Rice and poultry meat are major imported food items. Other imported products include machinery, fuel for vehicles, and cotton fabric. Haiti buys the most goods from the Dominican Republic, followed by the United States. Clothing is Haiti's largest **export**. About 85 percent of all Haitian exports go to the United States.

Since Haiti's 2010 earthquake, construction workers have been needed to rebuild homes, schools, hospitals, and offices.

Goods and Services BY THE NUMBERS

40% Portion of Haitian workers who do not have jobs.

About 35% Percentage of Haiti's imports that come from the Dominican Republic.

More Than $10 Million Value of Haiti's yearly mango exports.

INDIGENOUS PEOPLES

The first people to live on the island now called Hispaniola were **hunter-gatherers**. They sailed across the Caribbean Sea from Central or South America more than 5,000 years ago. About 3,000 years ago, another group of hunter-gatherers arrived. This group was called the Ciboney. They lived in caves and on small islands in western Haiti. The Ciboney made tools out of stone.

The Taíno arrived in Hispaniola around the year 300 BC. They spoke a language called Arawak, which began in present-day Venezuela. The Taíno often lived in large villages built in forest clearings. Houses were constructed around an open space where dancing, ball games, and religious ceremonies took place. The Taíno brought agriculture to Hispaniola. Their major crops were corn, cassava, and yams.

Indigenous Peoples BY THE NUMBERS

About 1,000 Miles
Distance traveled by the Taíno from what is now Venezuela to Haiti. (1,600 km)

3,000 Estimated number of people who lived in some Taíno villages.

100 Number of paddlers who could sit in a Taíno canoe.

Rock carvings thought to be done by Taíno people have been found on Hispaniola.

THE AGE OF EXPLORATION

December 6, 1492
Date Columbus and his crew first reached Hispaniola.

39 Number of sailors Columbus left at La Navidad after his first voyage.

30,000 Estimated Taíno population on Hispaniola 20 years after the first contact with Europeans in 1492.

Up to 3 million Taíno were living on Hispaniola when Columbus and his crew arrived in the late 15th century. Columbus named the island La Isla Española, which means "Spanish Island." Over time, the name changed to Hispaniola.

Columbus traded with the Taíno people he met. He and his crew built a fort on the island. They called the fort La Navidad. After Columbus sailed back to Europe, the fort was burned by the Taino, and the crew members he left there disappeared. However, other Spanish settlers would soon arrive.

Columbus had found gold on Hispaniola. Spain sent ships and people to mine the island's gold and take it to Europe. The Spanish forced Taíno men, women, and children to work as slaves in the gold mines. Almost all the Taíno on Hispaniola died following the arrival of Spanish settlers. Some Taíno were killed. Others died from the work conditions in the mines. The largest numbers died from new diseases the Spanish had brought from Europe.

When Columbus met the Taíno people, he gave them hawks' bells, small round bells that Europeans used to train birds for hunting.

EARLY SETTLERS

The French pirate François L'Olonais lived on the island of Tortuga. He attacked Spanish ships and settlements throughout the Caribbean.

During the 1500s, gold deposits in the Spanish mines on Hispaniola began to run low. Many Spaniards left the island. Most of those who remained lived in the east, in the present-day Dominican Republic. In the 1600s, French pirates moved into the area. French settlers followed. They set up forts and **plantations** on Hispaniola, mainly in the western part of the island. The French called the western region Saint-Domingue. They brought African slaves to the **colony**. The slaves worked on the plantations, growing sugarcane, coffee, and other crops.

By the late 1700s, more than 10 times as many slaves as Europeans lived in Saint-Domingue. The harsh living and working conditions led many slaves to struggle for freedom. Some escaped slaves, known as Maroons, gathered in the mountains, where they fought against French soldiers. Saint-Domingue also had a large population of people with mixed European and African origins. These people were known as Affranchis. They had more rights than slaves but fewer rights than Europeans. They too wanted equal rights.

After harvesting sugarcane, African slaves processed it to make sugar on Saint-Domingue's plantations.

Between 1791 and 1804, a series of wars and uprisings moved Saint-Domingue toward independence. The period is known as the Haitian Revolution. Slaves, Maroons, and Affranchis, sometimes aided by Spanish and British troops, all fought against the French.

In the late 1790s, a former slave named François Dominique Toussaint, also known as Toussaint Louverture, rose to power in Saint-Domingue. Two other leaders with African origins, Jean-Jacques Dessalines and Henry Christophe, were generals in Toussaint's army. In 1801, Toussaint invaded the Spanish eastern part of Hispaniola and gained control of the entire island. However, French troops invaded Saint-Domingue in 1801. Eventually, they captured Toussaint. Then, his former generals Dessalines and Christophe attacked and defeated the French army.

In 1804, the former French colony became an independent country, named Haiti. Dessalines became Haiti's first emperor, but he was killed during a revolt in 1806. Then, Christophe took power and became Haiti's king.

Toussaint fought the French with guerrilla warfare tactics, such as ambushes and hit-and-run attacks.

POPULATION

Haiti is home to more than 10 million people. The country's population increases by about 2 percent each year. Many Haitian families have several children. The population is not increasing more quickly because, in recent years, large numbers of Haitians have **emigrated**. Often, people leave to find work and better opportunities in countries such as the United States, the Dominican Republic, France, and Canada.

In terms of the age of the population, Haiti is a young country. More than half of Haitians are younger than 25 years old. This compares to less than one-third in the United States. The average **life expectancy** in Haiti is 64 years. This is 15 years less than the figure for the United States. Many Haitians are poor and often do not have access to medical care or healthful food.

About three out of five Haitians live in **urban** areas. More than 1.2 million people live in Port-au-Prince. Nearby cities are home to about 1 million more. These include Carrefour, Delmas, and Pétionville. Port-de-Paix, on the north coast, has about 250,000 people.

10,485,800
Estimated 2016 population of Haiti.

33%
Portion of the population that is under 15 years old.

More Than 600,000
Number of people born in Haiti who are living in the United States.

Many Haitians have tried to enter the United States without the proper papers, sailing to Florida in small, crowded boats.

POLITICS AND GOVERNMENT

In the period since Haiti gained its independence, the country has often been ruled by **dictators**. In 1957, François Duvalier, known as Papa Doc, named himself president for life and created a special force of soldiers to help him control the people. When Papa Doc died in 1971, his son Jean-Claude Duvalier, often called Baby Doc, took power. He also named himself president for life. However, widespread protests forced him to leave office in 1986.

Haiti's first fair, peaceful presidential election took place in 1990. Jean-Bertrand Aristide was elected president. Since then, there have been other fair elections and also other periods of harsh rule or violent protests following elections that seemed unfair.

Under Haiti's **constitution**, the president is elected for a five-year term. The legislature has two houses, the Senate and the Chamber of Deputies. The Supreme Court is Haiti's highest court.

2011 Year Haiti held its first election for president and members of the legislature after the destructive 2010 earthquake.

30 Number of members in Haiti's Senate.

118 Number of seats in the Chamber of Deputies.

Jean-Bertrand Aristide served as Haiti's president three times between 1990 and 2004.

CULTURAL GROUPS

About 95 percent of Haitians are black. Their **ancestors** were the slaves brought to Haiti by European settlers. The other 5 percent of Haitians are people of European origins or mulattoes, who have mixed African and European heritage.

Haiti's cuisine, or type of cooking, has been influenced by the different groups that helped form Haitian culture. Traditional French, Spanish, and African foods have shaped Haitian recipes. Often, locally grown foods such as mushrooms, rice, and peppers are combined with French-style sauces. The most common dish in Haiti is *riz et pois*. This name is French for rice and beans.

Fresh fish and plantains, a kind of banana used in cooking, are common ingredients in Haitian dishes.

Religion is an important part of life in Haiti. French and other European settlers brought the Roman Catholic faith to the area. Today, more than four-fifths of Haitians practice Roman Catholicism or another Christian faith.

Groups of Haitians dance in parades to celebrate Carnival, a festival leading up to the Christian holiday of Easter.

Haiti is also well known for the voodoo religion, sometimes spelled vodou. Voodoo grew out of the beliefs of African slaves in Haiti. People who follow voodoo believe that all things in the world are spirits. Many Haitians practice voodoo along with another religion.

Haiti has two official languages. They are French and Haitian Creole. French is the main language that is taught in schools. However, Haitian Creole is the most widely spoken language in the country.

Creole is often used by people in their day-to-day lives. It is also spoken in many formal situations, such as court cases and debates in the legislature. Haitian Creole developed in plantation settlements during colonial times. It is a combination of French and the various languages of Haiti's African slaves.

Bathers use a sacred pool in the annual voodoo festival that takes place across Haiti during Easter weekend.

ARTS AND ENTERTAINMENT

Haiti is home to a lively arts scene. The country's history and culture have influenced the works of all types of creative artists. Haitian painters, writers, musicians, and filmmakers are known around the world.

Well-known Haitian painters include John James Audubon, who was born in Haiti in 1785. His very detailed and accurate paintings of birds brought him world renown in both art and science. In the 20th century, painter Wilson Bigaud used bright colors to capture busy scenes of life in Haiti. Hector Hyppolite sometimes painted with his fingers or with chicken feathers to create his African-influenced art. Sculptor Georges Liautaud made his works out of metal. In 1944, Bigaud, Hyppolite, and Liautaud started the Centre d'Art in Port-au-Prince. The center displays the works of these and other artists, and it helps young Haitian artists become better known.

One of the birds Audubon painted was the roseate spoonbill, which still lives in parts of the southeastern United States.

Many present-day Haitian artists use bright colors and themes of daily life in their paintings.

Oswold Durand, who lived from 1840 to 1906, is one of Haiti's greatest poets. His poems describe the beauty of his home country and its people. Durand also wrote about problems in Haitian society and politics. In the 1930s and 1940s, the works of Jacques Roumain explored similar issues. His novel *Gouverneurs de la Rosée* is still popular in Haiti and around the world. Edwidge Danticat is one of Haiti's most celebrated modern writers. Danticat, who now lives in the United States, writes novels, short stories, and screenplays about her country's past.

Music is an important part of everyday life in Haiti. African, European, and other influences have been combined to form distinctly Haitian musical styles. One such style, kompa, joins African rhythms with European ballroom dance music. Haitian musicians such as Wyclef Jean, the hip-hop artist and member of the Fugees, have become popular around the world.

Haitian filmmakers such as Raoul Peck have created movies about Haiti's troubled history. Peck's film *The Man on the Shore* portrays Haiti during Papa Doc Duvalier's time in power. Peck's documentary *Fatal Assistance* describes the inefficiency of aid groups trying to help people in Haiti after the 2010 earthquake.

Arts and Entertainment BY THE NUMBERS

435 Number of bird paintings in John James Audubon's *Birds of America*, printed in the early 1800s.

More Than 15 Million
Number of copies sold worldwide of The Fugees' album *The Score*.

2008 Year Edwidge Danticat won the National Book Critics Circle Award for her autobiography *Brother, I'm Dying*.

The Port-au-Prince band RAM performs a kind of music called mizik rasin, a combination of folk music and rock-and-roll.

SPORTS

Soccer, called football in Haiti, is the most popular sport in the country. Haiti's top players compete in professional leagues and the country's national soccer program. Some Haitian players have become international stars.

In the mid-1900s, Joe Gaetjens became one of Haiti's best-known soccer players. In 1950, he played for the United States team in the World Cup tournament. That is soccer's international championship. During the tournament, Gaetjens scored the only goal in an upset U.S. victory over the favored British team.

Soveline Beaubrun began playing for Haiti's women's national soccer team in 2015.

Haiti's men's and women's national soccer teams represent the country in international tournaments. The men's team has qualified once, in 1974, for the World Cup tournament. The men's and women's teams both compete in tournaments for national teams based in the Americas.

The Haitian men's national soccer team, wearing blue uniforms, was one of 16 teams from the Americas that competed in the Copa America Centenario tournament, held in 2016 in the United States.

Haiti's large community in the United States has a strong influence on Haitian sports. American sports such as basketball and National Football League football are gaining popularity in Haiti. Olden Polynice was born in Port-au-Prince and moved to the United States. From 1987 to 2004, he spent 17 seasons playing professional basketball in the National Basketball Association (NBA). Samuel Dalemberts, also born in Port-au-Prince, played from 2001 to 2015 in the NBA, where he was nicknamed "The Haitian Sensation."

Some Haitians enjoy a type of martial arts called pinge. This sport is similar to wrestling. Pinge tournaments take place during the week before Easter. Bands play as the wrestlers compete.

Tennis and cycling are popular sports among wealthier people in Haiti. Equipment for these sports can be expensive. Swimming is a popular sport with many Haitians, and the country's climate makes it possible to enjoy outdoor swimming year-round.

Sports BY THE NUMBERS

2 Number of goals scored by Haiti in the 1974 World Cup.

1904 Year that the Haitian national men's soccer team was founded.

8,265 Number of points scored by Olden Polynice in his NBA career.

Samuel Dalembert played in 886 NBA games and scored a total of 6,814 points.

Mapping Haiti

We use many tools to interpret maps and to understand the locations of features such as cities, states, lakes, and rivers. The map below has many tools to help interpret information on the map of Haiti.

Map of Haiti

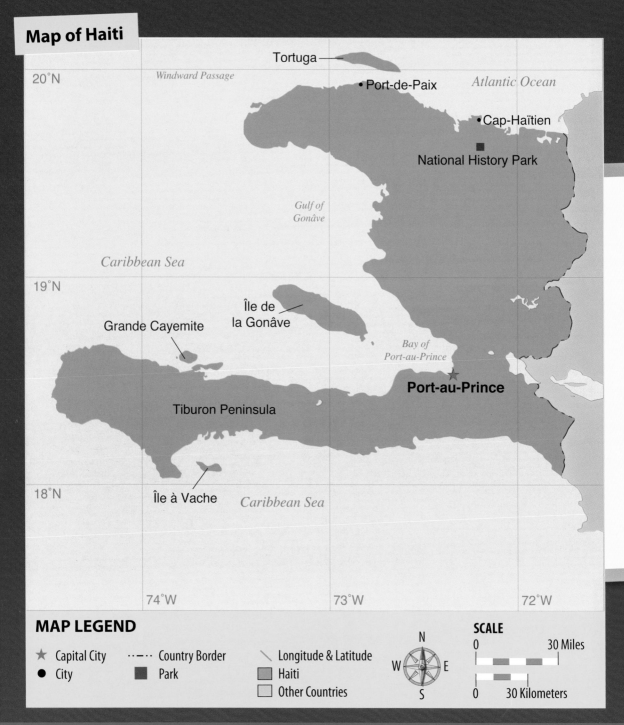

- Tortuga
- *Windward Passage*
- 20°N
- •Port-de-Paix
- *Atlantic Ocean*
- •Cap-Haïtien
- ■ National History Park
- *Gulf of Gonâve*
- *Caribbean Sea*
- 19°N
- Île de la Gonâve
- Grande Cayemite
- *Bay of Port-au-Prince*
- ★ **Port-au-Prince**
- Tiburon Peninsula
- 18°N
- Île à Vache
- *Caribbean Sea*
- 74°W
- 73°W
- 72°W

MAP LEGEND

★ Capital City	---·--- Country Border	╲ Longitude & Latitude
● City	■ Park	▨ Haiti
		▢ Other Countries

SCALE

0 ——— 30 Miles

0 ——— 30 Kilometers

N W E S

Mapping Tools

- The compass rose shows north, south, east, and west. The points in between represent northeast, northwest, southeast, and southwest.
- The map scale shows that the distances on a map represent much longer distances in real life. If you measure the distance between objects on a map, you can use the map scale to calculate the actual distance in miles or kilometers between those two points.

- The lines of latitude and longitude are long lines that appear on maps. The lines of latitude run east to west and measure how far north or south of the equator a place is located. The lines of longitude run north to south and measure how far east or west of the Prime Meridian a place is located. A location on a map can be found by using the two numbers where latitude and longitude meet. This number is called a coordinate and is written using degrees and direction. For example, the city of Port-au-Prince would be found at about 18°N and 72°W on a map.

Map It!

Using the map and the appropriate tools, complete the activities below.

Locating with latitude and longitude

1. Which island is located at 19°N and 73°W?
2. Which site is located at 20°N and 72°W?
3. Which city is found at 20°N and 73°W?

Distances between points

4. Using the map scale and a ruler, calculate the approximate distance between Port-au-Prince and Cap-Haïtien.
5. Using the map scale and a ruler, calculate the approximate distance between Tortuga and Île de la Gonâve.
6. Using the map scale and a ruler, calculate the approximate length of the Tiburon Peninsula.

ANSWERS 1. Île de la Gonâve 2. National History Park 3. Port-de-Paix 4. 80 miles (130 km) 5. 85 miles (135 km) 6. 130 miles (210 km)

Haiti 29

Quiz Time

Test your knowledge of Haiti by answering these questions.

1 What is the name of the island that includes Haiti?

2 What is Haiti's most popular sport?

3 Which former slave gained control of all of Hispaniola in 1801?

4 What is the name of Haiti's national bird?

5 What does Sans-Souci mean in French?

6 Which country receives the most exports from Haiti?

7 In what year did voodoo become an official religion in Haiti?

8 Who gave the island of Hispaniola the name La Isla Española?

9 What is the length of a president's term?

10 How many people live in Port-au-Prince?

ANSWERS

1. Hispaniola
2. Soccer
3. François Dominique Toussaint
4. Hispaniolan trogan
5. Without worry
6. United States
7. 2003
8. Christopher Columbus
9. Five years
10. More than 1.2 million

Key Words

ancestors: people in one's family or cultural group in past times

artifacts: objects made or changed by people in the past

bauxite: a mineral that contains the metal aluminum

colony: a country or area controlled by another country

constitution: a written document stating a country's or area's basic principles and laws

dictators: rulers who have absolute power and allow people very little freedom

emigrated: left one's country of origin to move to another country

endangered: at risk of becoming extinct, or dying out completely in the world or in an area

export: a product that is sold to other countries

gross domestic product: the total value of goods produced and services provided in a country during a year

habitat: the environment in which a plant or animal naturally lives

hunter-gatherers: people who obtain their food by hunting and by gathering foods found in nature

hydroelectricity: electricity produced using the energy of moving water

imported: bought from other countries

lagoons: small, shallow bodies of water connected to larger bodies of water

life expectancy: the number of years a person is expected to live

mammals: animals that have hair or fur and that feed mother's milk to their young

mausoleum: a large tomb

peninsulas: areas of land surrounded on three sides by water

plains: flat areas with few or no trees

plantations: large farms where one crop or a few crops are grown in order to be sold

plateau: an area of flat land at high elevation above sea level

species: groups of individuals with common characteristics

strait: a narrow water passage connecting two larger bodies of water

subsistence farming: a type of farming that provides food for the farm family, leaving little or nothing to sell

UNESCO: the United Nations Educational, Scientific, and Cultural Organization, whose main goals are to promote world peace and eliminate poverty through education, science, and culture

urban: relating to a city or town

Index

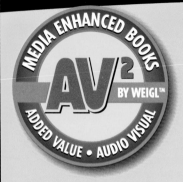

Log on to www.av2books.com

AV[2] by Weigl brings you media enhanced books that support active learning. Go to www.av2books.com, and enter the special code found on page 2 of this book. You will gain access to enriched and enhanced content that supplements and complements this book. Content includes video, audio, weblinks, quizzes, a slide show, and activities.

AV[2] Online Navigation

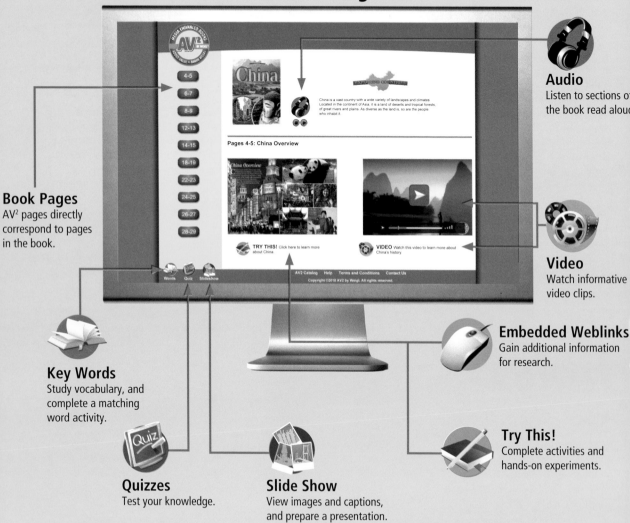

Audio
Listen to sections of the book read aloud

Book Pages
AV[2] pages directly correspond to pages in the book.

Video
Watch informative video clips.

Key Words
Study vocabulary, and complete a matching word activity.

Embedded Weblinks
Gain additional information for research.

Quizzes
Test your knowledge.

Slide Show
View images and captions, and prepare a presentation.

Try This!
Complete activities and hands-on experiments.

AV[2] was built to bridge the gap between print and digital. We encourage you to tell us what you like and what you want to see in the future.

Sign up to be an AV[2] Ambassador at www.av2books.com/ambassador.

Due to the dynamic nature of the Internet, some of the URLs and activities provided as part of AV[2] by Weigl may have changed or ceased to exist. AV[2] by Weigl accepts no responsibility for any such changes. All media enhanced books are regularly monitored to update addresses and sites in a timely manner. Contact AV[2] by Weigl at 1-866-649-3445 or av2books@weigl.com with any questions, comments, or feedback.